Lover of Life

F. W. Boreham's Tribute
to His Mentor

Lover of Life:
F. W. Boreham's Tribute to His Mentor

Lover of Life

F. W. Boreham's Tribute
to His Mentor

FRANK WILLIAM BOREHAM

John Broadbanks Publishing
Eureka, CA 2007

Published by John Broadbanks Publishing 2007

First Published in 1948 as
The Man Who Saved Gandhi by
The Epworth Press
London

ISBN 978-0-9790334-0-7

Printed in the United States of America

Contents

Foreword

This is a tantalizing sketch of Joseph John Doke, a Baptist Minister, artist and author, who was born in 1861 and ministered in England, New Zealand and South Africa. It is the stirring account of a frail man who became a fighter against discriminating legislation and an advocate with Mahatma Gandhi in championing the freedom of Indians in South Africa. As well as serving as pastor of the Johannesburg Baptist church, Doke participated in protests, contributed to newspapers and had the distinction of writing the first biography of Mahatma Gandhi.[1] In 1913 he visited Northern Rhodesia (now Zambia) to explore a new development for the South African Baptist Missionary Society and died tragically on his way home.

This book was published in 1948 and is sadly out of print and difficult to obtain. The decision has been taken to republish this book, not only to highlight the remarkable story of J. J. Doke but to provide an illustration of an effective mentoring relationship.

Nothing New about Mentoring

Many people today speak about mentoring as if it is a new phenomenon about which contemporary leaders should be engaged. It has been called by different names (supervision, curacy, spiritual director) but the practice has been around forever and was superbly practiced by J. J. Doke and F. W. Boreham. Instead of offering a treatise on effective mentoring, Boreham, in his inimitable way, tells stories of how it worked for him and how pivotal such a relationship was in his own life and ministry.

Relationship Begins

Like the man cured of leprosy that bothered to return to thank his Galilean healer, this book is Frank Boreham's tribute to his mentor. This supervisory relationship was neither arranged by the seminary nor established by denominational leaders. The link was birthed in friendship. A year after Boreham commenced his ministry in New Zealand his young fiancée from England's Theydon Bois, arrived by ship in Christchurch. Boreham had asked the Rev J. J. Doke of the Oxford Terrace Baptist church to conduct the wedding and along with the help of J. J. North, who served as best man, the knot was tied.

Pastoral Mentoring

Pastoral care was the foundation and enduring element of the mentoring relationship. J. J. Doke forged a strong friendship with both Stella and Frank and regularly made the long trek (250 miles!) from Christchurch to Mosgiel to visit them on their home soil. The Borehams went through some difficult periods of depression and ill health when Stella almost died. The pastoral care exercised by Doke through his visits and his letters was a lifeline. On hearing the news of Doke's untimely death in 1913 Boreham reflected, "He married me and helped me in more ways than I can tell. His friendship in our New Zealand days is one of my most cherished memories."2

Mentoring Based on Mutual Respect

After a month of formal ministry, the young pastor who was fresh out of Spurgeon's College, felt totally inadequate and therefore receptive to any help that he could get. Boreham wrote, "I was just beginning and was hungry for any crumb of wisdom that he, out of his rich experience, could impart."3 It was this cry for help and his utmost respect for J. J. Doke that deepened the relationship. Boreham observed that Doke was "a born preacher"4 and on another occasion he said, "I have never known his equal as a preacher."5 What amazed Boreham was that his mentor had never received a College and seminary education, yet, "thanks to an indomitable will and tireless application, he was one of the most cultured and capable ministers I have ever known."6 Doke was ten years older than Boreham but the younger man never felt like the lesser partner.

Inspirational Mentoring

In this book F. W. Boreham attributes his 'conversion' to reading to the encouragement of J. J. Doke. As he advised Boreham to read widely and commit himself to studying at least one serious book a week, J. J. Doke gently coaxed the young pastor out of his narrowness and broadened him in dimensions beyond the pastoral role. As a lover of life he increased Boreham's appreciation of nature (Doke was seldom seen without his camera), and he enlarged his worldview. Doke was "an incorrigible traveler"[7] who undoubtedly passed on the travel bug to Boreham and reminded him of the ways travel can make one a more interesting person. It is instructive to see how Boreham like his mentor became a prolific letter writer and a regular contributor to newspapers.

The Broadening Role of the Mentor

It is fascinating to read the articles and correspondence that arose from Doke's period in Africa, especially concerning the close friendship that developed between him and Mahatma Gandhi.[8] The letters not only illustrate Doke's well-rounded ministry, but they provide a glimpse into the way his mentoring helped young Boreham to develop the important social and prophetic dimensions of Christian ministry, aspects that had been lacking in his early spiritual tutelage.

It is reassuring to witness the renaissance of mentoring in many walks of life but especially in the vocation of pastoral leadership. Such a relationship, if worked at, can be pastorally supportive, useful in integrating seminary training with practical ministry and vital in building accountability.

It would be good if seminary and denominational leaders put this book into the hands of every seminary student and pastor embarking on a new mentoring relationship. This short story about the friendship between J. J. Doke and Frank and Stella Boreham provides a wealth of insight and a hopeful vision of what a mentoring relationship might become.

Geoff Pound

Strangers in a
Strange Land

As a small boy I took for granted that Paul's famous phrase about entertaining angels unawares was a piece of pure hyperbole, a poetical expression coined as an incentive to hospitality. Soon after our marriage in New Zealand, however, my wife and I discovered that this glittering gem of apostolic diction represents a nugget of stark and sober fact.

We were ridiculously young, she and I, when we built our first home at Mosgiel in New Zealand: she was still in her teens. New Zealand, too, was young: we were able to chat, every day of our lives, with men and women who had come out on the very first emigrant ships. Strangers in so strange a land, we struggled bravely to make ourselves at home. And, on the whole, we managed fairly well until Christmas came. But when Christmas came in the hot blaze of midsummer, the fields around us aglow with golden harvests, it was too much for us. We felt wretchedly lonely and horribly homesick. Well meaning people wished us a merry Christmas. As if anybody could be merry under such conditions!

In those far-off days, however, it was our ineffable delight to welcome to our manse one happy guest who invariably brought his Christmas with him. Whenever he entered our

Mosgiel manse, every room echoed with the Glory to God in the Highest of the Bethlehem angels; and, whenever the front-door bell rang, we half suspected that, out in front of the house, we should see the Wise Men with their train of camels.

The man who set the angels singing in the Mosgiel manse was Joseph John Doke. Although one of the most dynamic and colorful personalities who ever spent a few years beneath these mistral stars, he was of so modest and unassuming a disposition that those within whose minds the mention of his name now awakens any responsive vibrations must be exceedingly few. And of those who were privileged to enjoy his companionship, scarcely anybody suspected that his whole life was an epic of romance and adventure.

It chanced that in 1894, two churches in New Zealand needed ministers. The city pulpit at Christchurch was vacant; and the little church at Mosgiel, that had never indulged in a minister before, resolved with great trepidation to venture on the momentous experiment. Both sent to England. Mr. Doke was appointed to Christchurch, and I, fresh from college, was allocated to Mosgiel. And so we met in Maori-Land; and, as the first of the many notable services that he rendered me, he officiated at my wedding.

Magnetic Personality

J.J.D., as we affectionately called him—although the natives of Central Africa knew him as Shikulu Dolco was one of two brothers, the sons of the first minister of the Baptist Church at Chudleigh in Devonshire. Both boys early imbibed a sincere faith in Christ and a fervent enthusiasm for the evangelization of the world. The elder volunteered for the Congo, and, almost as soon as he arrived, laid down his life there. The tragic circumstance profoundly affected the mind of the surviving brother. He remembered how, when Thomas Knibb died at the very inception of his missionary venture in Jamaica, his brother William, who had cherished no overseas ambitions, immediately took the vacant place. But the cases were not parallel. With the Knibbs, it was the weaker brother who died, leaving the stronger to succeed him. But, with the Dokes, it was the more robust brother who perished, leaving the other unequal to the coveted task. Joseph would gladly have gone out to the scene of his brother's sacrifice, but, though possessed of the essential spirit and the requisite gifts, his health was far too frail. Notwithstanding his alert mind, his hunger for knowledge and his winsome personality, the doctors would not hear of his taking a college course. He abandoned with a sigh his

African dream; but the fact that, years afterwards, he named all his children after heroes of the Congo mission field, indicate unmistakably the emotions that still held all his heart.

But although the colleges were closed against him, no power on earth could have kept him out of a pulpit. He was a born preacher. Looking back over a fairly long life, I affirm deliberately that, for the natural eloquence that can stir men's deepest emotions and sweep an audience off its feet, I have never known his equal. For some years he held his brittle body and his shining soul together by occupying a pulpit for a few months, saving every penny that he possibly could, and then spending the proceeds on an excursion or a cruise.

On all these gipsyings, he became the idol of his fellow-travelers. He was lounging one evening on the deck of a P. and O. liner in the Mediterranean when the captain, taking the empty chair beside him, asked him if he was on his way to the Holy Land. Mr. Doke, who had only saved enough money for the return trip to Port Said, explained that he was going straight back. Guessing the reason, the captain ridiculed the idea. "Nonsense!" he laughed, "you're going on! Now look at me! I'm the skipper of a liner, having nobody on earth on whom to spend my salary! You go on; see all that there is to be seen in Palestine; and you'll make me happy for the rest of my life!"

I remember, too, his telling me of a bitterly cold night that he was forced to spend on a lonely wayside station in India. "My only companion," he said, "was a tall Bengali, rolled up in a rug on a wooden seat, fast asleep. I paced the platform to keep warm. At last I was compelled to lie down for a minute and must have dozed. For, when I awoke, I was snugly wrapped up in the rug and the Indian was walking up and down to keep warm!" In the fine biography of my old friend, written by Mr. W. E. Cursons, we catch glimpses of him in South Africa, in Ceylon, in America and in many odd corners of the planet; and, everywhere, he exercised his resistless magnetism on everyone he met.

Lover of Life

At last, convinced that two years spent in the dry air of the African Karoo had patched up the holes in his lungs, he married a very charming girl at Graaf-Reinet and returned to England to succeed his father at his birthplace. After two years at Chuddigh and five at Bristol, he turned his face to the Antipodes. And so we met. At first glance we felt sorry for him. He was so small and so frail; he looked at times as if a puff of wind would blow him away. His asthma racked him pitilessly, day and night. Yet he never behaved as a sick man; never, if he could possibly help it, referred to his weakness. In all his movements he was brisk, vigorous, sprightly. He thought health; assumed health; radiated health. He emerged from his room every morning with the sunniest of smiles; whilst, long before breakfast was over, his clever witticisms and excellent stories would have everybody in the best of humor. His comments on the morning's paper represented a liberal education. His mind was so richly stored that every item in the news drew from him striking comparisons and dramatic contrasts gathered from the storied past.

The outlook from each window captivated him. As often as not, he would draw his sketch-book from his breast pocket and limn some pretty peep that particularly took his fancy. His home was luxuriously beautified by the multitude of his oil-paintings. When he slipped out into the garden, every flower, insect and bird awoke his enthusiasm. He loved life— life in every form and phase. In his later days he established a little zoo of his own and filled the house with the strangest pets. He would tell me in his letters of his lemurs, his meer-cats and his monkeys, and of the many-colored birds in his aviary. And, as though real life failed to satisfy him, he invaded the realm of fiction. He wrote two novels—stories of the Karoo—that, for mystery and adventure, have been compared with the fancies of Rider Haggard. His lust of life was insatiable. I seldom saw him without his camera. He was eager to perpetuate every scene that confronted him, every experience that befell him.

Conversion to
Serious Reading

Nothing contributed more to the happiness and enrichment of our lives at Mosgiel than his visits to our manse. I was ten years his junior. Whilst never making me feel that he was presuming upon his seniority, he always impressed me as being intensely anxious that I should acquire, without the toil of patient and laborious search, the intellectual and spiritual wealth that he had gathered in the course of those extra years of pilgrimage. Seated on the broad and sunlit veranda of my Mosgiel manse, he would pour the golden treasure of his mind and heart into my hungry ear. All that he had learned about the choice of books, about systems of study, about the conduct of public worship, about the art of preaching, and about the best method of pastoral visitation, he endeavored, in its entirety, to impart to me.

He was particularly anxious about my library and the use I made of its contents. In the absence of a college education, he owed everything to the books that he had privately purchased and devoured. "Read, my dear man," he exclaimed, one day, springing to his feet in his excitement and pacing the veranda in his characteristic way, "Read; and read systematically; and keep on reading; never give up!"

"But give me a start," I pleaded, "be definite; what shall I read first?" He walked the whole length of the veranda and back without replying. Then, approaching me with eyes that positively burned, he cried with tremendous emphasis: "Begin with Gibbon! Read Gibbon through and through! Don't drop it because the first volume seems dry! Keep right on, and you'll soon have no time for bed and no inclination to sleep even if you go there!"

I bought Gibbon's *Decline and Fall of the Roman Empire* the very next day. I would give a king's ransom, always assuming that I possess such a thing, to recapture the wild excitement of that magnificent adventure. It was my first serious incursion into the world of books. In my boyhood and youth I had read hundreds of books; books, for the most part, about pirates, Red Indians and grizzly bears, followed by a shelf or two of love stories and other romances of a sentimental kind. But what was this to the glory of Gibbon? I have the volumes still; and if, one of these days, I have either to sell them or starve, I tremble to think that I may by that time have fallen so low as to consent to their sacrifice. None of the tales of smuggler caves, or escapes in the jungle, or fights with sheiks and cannibals had ever fired my fancy as Gibbon did. Every chapter seemed to be a more gorgeous painting and a more spacious canvas than the one that preceded it. My imagination was so captivated by the swaying hordes of Goths and Huns, Vandals and Saracens that I started in my sleep as this imposing and variegated pageant of martial movement swept majestically through my dreams. My unfortunate and long-suffering little congregation was dumfounded by the discovery that, whether the text were taken from Psalm or Gospel or Epistle, it could only be effectively expounded by copious references to the Avars, the Sabians, the Moguls and the Lombards, and could only he successfully illustrated by romantic stories about the hermits, the caliphs, the crusaders and the monks. Roman emperors stalked majestically through every prayer meeting address. Mosgiel was as astonished as ancient Gaul had been at finding itself suddenly invaded by the Roman legions! Poor little congregation! They did not suspect that their young minister had burst upon a new planet and that his brain was all in a whirl at the splendor of the discoveries that he was daily making!

Doors Opening

For me, this intensive study of Gibbon, under Mr. Doke's supervision, led to a sequel that has colored all my days. For, before I had finished the final volume, I found myself late one night in the office of Mr. (afterwards Sir) George Fenwick, the editor of the Otago Daily Times. I discovered that Mr. Fenwick was toying with the idea of inviting me to write leading articles on special subjects, for his paper. "Tomorrow's leader has yet to be written," he remarked; "if you had to write it, what would you say?"

It chanced that, at that moment, all the young men in New Zealand were struggling to join the contingents that were being dispatched to South Africa. This historic development exactly synchronized with my excitement over Gibbon. "If I were writing tomorrow's leader," I replied, with confidence, "I should establish a contrast between the patriotic eagerness of these young men to serve in South Africa and the shameful reluctance of young Romans to defend the Empire in the days of its decline and fall." "That sounds promising," Mr. Fenwick replied; "suppose you sit down and write it!"

Next morning, in the big kitchen of the Mosgiel manse, a young minister and his wife gazed upon the leading article in that day's paper with a pride such as Lucifer can never have known. Thus Gibbon, my first purchase under Mr. Doke's scheme paid for himself, as most of my books have done. For, from that hour, at Mr. Fenwick's invitation, I wrote leading articles for the Otago Daily Times on all kinds of historical, scientific and literary themes. And, after leaving New Zealand I found ample scope for similar service on other daily papers. I have written more than two thousand leading articles in all. Many of these have become the germs from which the essays published in my books have subsequently developed. When Mr. Fenwick received his knighthood, he assured me, in acknowledging my sincere felicitations, that he had often smiled over the recollection of our chat in his office on that bitter winter's night in the long, long ago.

Striking the Deeper Note

Nine times out of ten, before we rose from our chairs after these heart-to-heart talks, J.J.D. would strike a deeper note. How can a minister keep his soul in rapt communion with God? How can he inflame his personal devotion to his Savior? How can he ensure the indwelling of the gracious Spirit? How can he prevent the evaporation of his early consecration, the fading of his youthful ideals? How can he keep his faith fresh, his passion burning, and his vision dear? When my companion turned to such topics, as he so often did, his eyes lit up, his soul shone in his face; he would lean forward in his chair in an ecstasy of fervor; he would talk like a man inspired.

For J.J.D. represented in his own person the most engaging and most lovable type of masculine saintliness of which I have ever had personal experience. He literally walked with God. He dwelt in the secret place of the Most High and abode under the shadow of the Almighty. God was never far away when he was near. To him the study of the Bible was a ceaseless revelry. During his earlier ministry he read it, from cover to cover, four times a year.

Role Play

Irecall a day on which the three of us, the Mistress of the Manse, Mr. Doke and I, had just finished afternoon tea on the lawn. We were still toying with our cups when a young fellow rode up on a bicycle. Taking me aside, he told me that Nellie Gillespie, a member of my young people's Bible class, was sinking fast: it was unlikely that she would last the night. As soon as the messenger had left, I explained the position to Mr. Doke, and begged him to excuse me. "Of course," he replied, "but, first, come and sit here beside me." He threw himself full length in the lounge chair, his body almost horizontal. "See," he said, "I am Nellie Gillespie. I am just about to die. I have sent for you. What have you to say to me?"

Entering into the spirit of the thing, I leaned towards him and unfolded to him the deathless story that I shortly intended to pour into the ears of the real Nellie Gillespie. "Oh, my dear sir," he moaned, "you're saying far too much. It's almost as bad as a theological lecture. Remember I'm utterly exhausted, months of languishing consumption . . . I shall be gone in an hour or two. Make it very short and very simple."

I began again, condensing into a few sentences all that I had said before. "Shorter still," he demanded; "shorter and simpler! Remember, I'm dreadfully tired and weak. Shorter and simpler!"

I made a third venture, telling in just a word or two of the eternal Love and the eternal Cross. "Splendid!" he cried, springing suddenly to his feet and clasping my hand. "Now away you go, as quickly as you can; and remember, whilst you are praying with Nellie Gillespie, I shall be praying for you! God bless you!" And the next day he assisted me at Nellie's funeral.

Wise Counselor

One lovely morning we were sitting together on the veranda, looking away across the golden plains to the purple and sunlit mountains, when I submitted to him a very pertinent question: "Can a man be quite sure," I asked, "that, in the hour of perplexity, he will be rightly led? Can he feel secure against a false step?" I shall never forget his reply. He sprang from his deck chair and came earnestly towards me. "I am certain of it," he exclaimed, "if he will but give God time! Remember that as long as you live," he added, entreatingly. "Give God time!"

Ten years later, Mr. Doke having left New Zealand in the interval, my wife and I found ourselves in the throes of a terrible perplexity. I had received a call to Hobart in Tasmania. It took us completely by surprise: I knew nobody in Tasmania and nobody in Tasmania knew me. The thought of leaving Mosgiel nearly broke my heart: I loved every stick and stone about the place. But I was compelled to recognize that Hobart, being a city, offered opportunities of influence that Mosgiel could never boast.

The call came in 1906. In 1903 the Mosgiel Church had presented us with a delightful trip to the dear Homeland, a heavy undertaking for so small a congregation. Could I, after accepting such munificence at their hands, think of leaving them? If my call to Hobart had been public property, I could have consulted my officers on the point. But not a soul knew of it, and we thought it best to keep the secret to ourselves until our decision had been taken.

For reasons of their own, the officials at Hobart had asked me to let them have my decision not later than a certain Saturday, three weeks distant, and I had promised to respect their wishes in that matter. As that day drew nearer, the issues narrowed themselves down to one. Did the acceptance of the English trip commit me to a prolonged ministry at Mosgiel?

When that Saturday dawned, we were as far from finality as ever. The post office closed at five o'clock in the afternoon and I was determined, come what might, to hand in my reply by then. In my confusion I recalled for my comfort that memorable conversation on the veranda ten years earlier. Give God time! But I had not much more time to give. That Saturday afternoon, to add to our distress, a visitor arrived. She stayed until half-past four. "Come on," I then said to my wife, "put on your hat and we'll walk down to the post office. We must send the telegram by five o'clock, whatever happens."

At five minutes to five we were standing together in the porch of the post office, desperately endeavoring to make up our minds. We were giving God time: would the guidance come? At three minutes to five, Gavin, the church secretary, rode up on a bicycle. He was obviously agitated.

"What do you think I heard in the city this morning?" he asked eagerly. I assured him that I could form no idea.

"Well," he replied, his news positively sizzling on his tongue, "I heard that you have been called to Hobart!"

"It's true enough, Gavin," I answered, "but how can we consider such an invitation after your goodness in giving us a trip to England?"

"A trip to England!" he almost shouted. "Man alive, didn't you earn your trip to England before you went? Why, you're very nearly due for another!"

I begged him to excuse me a moment. The clerk at the counter was preparing to close the office. I handed in my telegram and rejoined Gavin, who insisted on taking us home to tea. At his house I wrote out my resignation, asking him to call the officers together at ten o'clock next morning. And although the emotional strain under which I found myself choked my utterance and compelled me to leave to Gavin the task of explanation, I felt, beyond the shadow of doubt, that the promised guidance had not failed me and that Mr. Doke's assurance had been amply vindicated.

Discoverer of Nonsense

Mr. Doke was a natural humorist. I shall never forget the triumphs that he achieved by his faculty for fun. I never knew a man in whom holiness and humor blended as they did in him. I have known many good men who loved to laugh; but the goodness and the laughter seemed somehow to dwell in separate compartments of their being. When they were laughing you temporarily forgot their devoutness; and when they were praying you forgot their peals of merriment. But with Mr. Doke it was quite otherwise. The ingredients, both of his humor and of his piety, were such that they blended most perfectly, and you could never tell where the one ended and the other began. And this remarkable trait was used by him for all it was worth.

It happened that Mr. Doke's sojourn in New Zealand synchronized with a trying period of storm and stress in the history of our Missionary Society. It was a most grave and anxious time for all of us, and I shall never forget how, time after time, his tactful wit would save a most delicate and threatening situation. Mr. Chesterton says that the discovery of nonsense was the greatest revelation of the nineteenth century. That being so, Mr. Doke deserves to be ranked as one of our greatest discoverers, for he saw, as few men saw, the inestimable value of that magic and potent force.

I can recall occasions when we had been sitting for hours anxiously discussing a depressing and apparently impossible situation, until our patience was exhausted, and our nerves unstrung. Out of sheer weariness and vexation we might easily have committed any sort of indiscretion. But over there in the corner sits Mr. Doke. He is taking out his pencil. In a moment or two, he has finished his work. With a few deft strokes he has, struck off an irresistibly comical cartoon, caricaturing some ridiculous phase in the trying affair, and focusing, in the drollest possible way, the humorous side of the knotty question. The cartoon was handed round, and we laughed immoderately over the product of Mr. Doke's captivating genius. A new atmosphere straightway enveloped the debate. The interruption was as refreshing as an hour's sleep or a delicious cup of tea. It was as though, a window having been opened in a stuffy room, the place had suddenly been filled with fresh and perfume-laden air. We settled down to work again with clearer brains, cheerier hearts and sweeter tempers.

Stilling Stormy Waters

This was in Committee; but he waved the same magic wand over the assembly. I remember a very painful debate that took place in those trying days. The question was as to whether or not certain letters should have been written. Some telling speeches had been made, and feeling was running very high. At length the time for voting arrived, and it looked as though the assembly would not only censure its officers, but perhaps precipitate a cleavage that many years would scarcely heal. The chairman rose to put the motion. The atmosphere was distinctly electrical and charged with tensest feeling.

In the nick of time, Mr. Doke cried, "Mr. President," and came striding down the aisle. I can see him now as he turned to address us. "Mr. President," he said, "is it not possible that both sides are right? Is it not possible that we are each reading into these troublesome letters our own strong feeling?

Let me tell you a story. Once upon a time a man had two children, a boy and a girl. In course of time, the boy became refractory and ran away from home. He was not heard of again for many years. The girl remained at her father's side and was his constant stay and comforter. Just as the old man had given up all hope of again hearing from his son, a letter arrived. But neither father nor daughter had been to school and they could not read it."

"Let us take it down to the butcher, father!" the daughter suggested. "He can read, and he will tell us what Tom say." To the butcher they accordingly hastened. Now, the butcher was a gruff, sour, surly old man, and they were unfortunate enough to find him in one of his nastiest moods. He tore open the letter with a grunt, withdrew it from its envelope and read: "Dear father, I'm very ill; send me some money, Yours, Tom." "The rascal!" the old man exclaimed indignantly, "he only wants my money. He shan't have a single penny!" They turned away sorrowfully, and set off towards home. But, on the way, another thought visited the daughter. "Father," she said, "What do you say to going to the baker? The butcher may have made a mistake. The baker can read, too; and he is a kind, Christian man. Let us go to him!" And to the baker's they went. Now the baker was a genial, gracious soul, with a voice tremulous with feeling and resonant with sympathy. He gently took the letter from its envelope and read: "Dear father, I'm very ill; send me some money, Yours, Tom" "The poor boy," the old man cried, brushing away a tear, "how much can we send him?"

The whole assembly was in the best of good humor at once. The application was obvious. It was as though the lowering thundercloud had broken in refreshing summer rain. The air was cleared, and the flowers were exhaling their choicest fragrance in the sunshine that followed the storm. Mr. Doke's beautiful personality had cast its spell over us all. We felt that we wanted an interval in which to shake hands with each other. He made a suggestion in closing that would obviate all risk of further complications. Both sides snatched at it eagerly; and the painful episode closed with expressions of the most cordial goodwill.

Sword Bathed in Heaven

He was a past master at this sort of thing. His sword, as the prophet would say, was bathed in heaven. He could rebuke in such a way that the person corrected felt as if a compliment had been paid him. I remember how, at Wellington, when he was President of the Conference, a deputation from the other churches of the city attended to convey fraternal greetings. It was at the end of a long session. I suppose we were weary and off our guard. Anyhow, we kept our seats as our visitors walked up the aisle to the rostrum. Mr. Doke was, of course, standing to receive them, shaking hands with each as they mounted the dais. "Brethren," he then exclaimed, "every man in this standing assembly welcomes you!" We sprang to our feet feeling very much ashamed of ourselves, and profited by the reproof on every similar occasion in the days that followed.

Natural Grace

I once accompanied him to a social function to which a young minister had brought the girl to whom he was engaged. The minister was walking about the hall chatting to his numerous friends, his prospective bride was sitting with a group of ladies in a corner. The minister, being well-known, was quickly supplied with a cup of coffee. He was just about to lift it to his lips when Mr. Doke intervened. Taking his hand, Mr. Doke gently led him to the corner in which his lady-love was seated. "Oh, Miss Pemberton," he exclaimed, "I'm afraid they're a little slow in serving the coffee, but Mr. Swain has managed to secure you a cup. And how are you enjoying yourself?" And so on. He did this kind of thing with such perfect ease and such natural grace that a rap on the knuckles from him felt for all the world like a caress.

Pair of Champions

It was after he left New Zealand, to the great sorrow of us all, that he made history. And, characteristically, he did it in such a way that, to this day, very few people realize the effect of his behavior on world affairs. He settled as minister at Johannesburg; and it so happened that, shortly afterwards, Mr. Gandhi went to South Africa as the legal representative of the Indian population, who, just then, were involved in a serious clash with the authorities. Mr. Doke's sympathies were with the Indians, and he immediately got into touch with Mr. Gandhi. Each were astonished at the other's diminutive stature. They did not look like a pair of champions. Mr. Doke says that he expected to see 'a tall and stately figure and a bold masterful face.' Instead of this, a small, little, spare figure stood, before me, and a refined, earnest face looked into mine. "The skin was dark, the eyes dark, but the smile which lighted up the face, and that direct, fearless glance, simply took one's heart by storm. I judged him to be about thirty-eight years of age, which proved correct. But the strain of his work showed its traces in the sprinkling of silver hairs on his head. He spoke English perfectly, and was evidently a man of great culture."

On the wall of Mr. Gandhi's office hung a beautiful picture of Jesus; and the moment that Mr. Doke's eyes rested upon it, he felt that he and his new friend were bound by a most sacred tie. "I want you," he said to Mr. Gandhi, "to consider me your friend in this struggle. If," he added, with a glance at the picture on the wall, "if I have learned any lesson from the life of Jesus it is that one should share and lighten the load of those who are heavily laden."

The days that followed were full of anxiety and even of peril. Indeed, they almost culminated in a tragedy that would have shocked the world. "I distinctly remember," Mr. Doke says, "that, as I went through the streets that morning, I was led to pray that I might be guided completely to do God's will; but I little thought what the answer would be." A few minutes later, a young Indian dashed up, gesticulating excitedly: "Come quick!" he cried. "Coolie, he hit Mr. Gandhi!" Following the Indian's footsteps, Mr. Doke found Mr. Gandhi lying in a pool of blood, looking half-dead. It turned out that a party of Pathans, taking it into their heads that Mr. Gandhi was seeking to betray the Indian cause, had plotted to destroy him. After bathing and bandaging his wounds, Mr. Doke asked the wounded man whether he would prefer to be taken to a hospital or to the manse. Mr. Gandhi gratefully accepted the latter alternative.

"Mr. Doke and his good wife," writes Mr. Gandhi, in telling the story, "were anxious that I should be perfectly at rest. They therefore removed all persons from near my bed. I made a request that their daughter, Olive, who was then only a little girl, should sing for me my favorite English hymn, 'Lead Kindly Light.' Mr. Doke liked this very much. He called Olive and asked her to sing in low tone. The whole scene passes before my eyes as I recall it. How shall I describe the service rendered me by the Doke family?

"Every day marked an advance in our mutual affection and intimacy. Naturally, after I was injured, all classes of Indians flocked to the house, from the humblest street-hawker, with dirty clothes and dusty boots, to the highest Indian officials.

"Mr. Doke would receive them all in his drawing-room with uniform courtesy and consideration. The whole family gave their time, either to nursing me or else receiving the hundreds of Indian visitors who came to see me. Even at night Mr. Doke would twice or thrice tiptoe into my room to see if I wanted anything."

Dream Fulfilled

Some years later, J.J.D. having died in the interval, Mr. Gandhi revisited South Africa in the company of the Rev. C. F. Andrews. "As we approached Johannesburg," says Mr. Andrews, Mr. Gandhi turned to me and said: "Charlie, I want to take you on a pilgrimage." "What do you mean?" I asked him, not following his line of thought. "I want you," he said, "to go with me to the house of Mrs. Doke, where I was nursed back to life."

"When we came to the house it was difficult for him to restrain his emotion, as he for the first time saw Mrs. Doke in her widow's dress and tried to comfort her. She, on her part, treated him with all the tenderness of a mother, forgetting her own sorrow in her anxiety about his health and that of Mrs. Gandhi, who was very ill.

"Mrs. Doke then related to us the story of the death of her husband in the interior of Africa." And the story that Mrs. Doke unfolded to her visitors is the story that I must myself set down before I lay aside my pen.

The amazing thing is that, in defiance of the physical frailty that had dogged his days, Mr. Doke laid his bones in a missionary grave after all! His brother's resting-place on the banks of the Congo always held a conspicuous place in the landscape of his life. I cannot stifle a suspicion that it was one of the factors that lured him to the adventure that glorified the close of his career.

He conceived the idea that it would enormously enrich the spirituality and increase the effectiveness of his own church at Johannesburg, and of all the South African churches, if they had a specific missionary objective, and especially an African objective. He talked it over with Fred Arnot, the renowned explorer and evangelist. Arnot told him of a lonely mission-station away up in the interior, not far from the upper reaches of the Congo, that might be taken over by the South African churches and made the center from which a vast unevangelized territory might be worked. The idea captivated Mr. Doke's imagination, and he felt sure that it would appeal to all the heroic instincts in the young men and women of the churches. With boyish excitement he resolved to set out on a great trek into the heart of the continent. Clement, his son, agreed to, accompany him. "We are off for the Congo Border," he wrote enthusiastically. "Is it a holiday trip? It seems a long way to go for a holiday. I would claim that we are prospectors, but it would be misunderstood. Yet that is really what we are—prospecting for missions." They set out on July 2, 1913. Infected by his ardor, his people crowded down to wave their affectionate farewells, and eagerly anticipated the stirring story that he would have to tell on his return.

His journal, carefully kept to the last, reads like a section of Livingstone's *Missionary Travels* or Stanley's *In Darkest Africa.* Here, as in those classics, we have the swamp and the jungle, the long grass and the winding trails, the lions and the hyenas, the zebras and the impalas, the mosquitoes and the tsetse flies.

His attempts to make the natives of the various villages understand his message are strangely reminiscent of Livingstone. The travelers reached their objective and were given a boisterous welcome: "Clement was almost overpowered and our ears tingled with the noise." They spent some days in conference with the missionaries; explored the entire area; and Mr. Doke formulated his plans for the establishment of his new scheme.

The return journey was more trying. But they bravely survived the ordeal of the long march, and, on August 5, reached the railway. Here father and son separated. Mr. Doke had promised, before terminating his travels, to visit a mission-station at Umtali, in Eastern Rhodesia. At Bulawayo, therefore, the two reluctantly parted, Clement taking the train home to Johannesburg and Mr. Doke turning his face towards Umtali.

And at Umtali he suddenly collapsed and died. "This is the time," he murmured, "when a man wants his wife." "Yes," replied Mr. Wodehouse, his missionary-host, "but One is near you who is better than wife or mother." "Yes," he replied. "I know that the Everlasting Arms are around me." He asked Mr. Wodehouse to pray with him; then to stroke his hair; and, later still, to hold his hand. And on Friday evening, August 15, 1913, he quietly and peacefully passed away.

Enduring Legacy

His life-work was, however, splendidly complete. His dream was more than realized. The work of that mission-station in the far north, to which his own children were among the first to dedicate their lives has prospered and developed in most unexpected ways. And, to this day, his memory, like a fragrance, pervades hundreds of homes on all five of the world's great continents.

Notes

1. J. J. Doke, *M. K. Gandhi: An Indian Patriot in South Africa* (London: London Indian Chronicle, 1909).
2. F. W. Boreham, *The Golden Milestone*, (London: The Epworth Press, 1915), 50.
3. F. W. Boreham, *The Ivory Spires*, (London: The Epworth Press, 1934), 29.
4. F. W. Boreham, *The Man Who Saved Gandhi*, (London: The Epworth Press), 5.
5. F. W. Boreham, *I Forgot To Say*, (London: The Epworth Press, 1948), 134.
6. F. W. Boreham, *The Ivory Spires*, 28-29.
7. F. W. Boreham, *The Passing of John Broadbanks*, (London: The Epworth Press, 1936), 200.
8. Joseph John Doke Biography, http://www.unisa.ac.za/Default.asp?Cmd=ViewContent&ContentID=11685, viewed 20 February 2006. Gandhi and South Africa http://www.anc.org.za/ancdocs/history/people/gandhi/1-4.htm, viewed 20 February 2006.

Publisher's Note

We are grateful to Dr. Frank Rees at Whitley College for the permission to republish this book and for the practical support given by the College. Permission to reproduce significant portions of this book can be obtained from Whitley College, 271 Royal Parade, Parkville, Australia, 3052.

A portion of the sale of each book will go toward the training of pastors and missionaries at Whitley College, a ministry that F. W. Boreham supported during his lifetime.

We appreciate the blessing of the Methodist Publishing House (successors of The Epworth Press) which previously published this book in 1948 under the title, *The Man Who Saved Gandhi: A Short Biography of John Joseph Doke.*

Sincere thanks to Laura Zugzda for her outstanding cover design.

This is the first effort by the newly formed John Broadbanks Publishing which aims to republish some of the out of print publications by F. W. Boreham and repackage some of the best of his writings for the growing number of readers interested in Boreham's writings.

If you would like to assist in the publishing of Boreham's writings, please make your donation payable to "Michael Dalton," and mail it to the address below.

Further information about the life and work of F. W. Boreham is available on the Internet at *The Official F. W. Boreham Blog Site* <http://fwboreham.blogspot.com>

Comments and questions can be addressed to:

Michael Dalton
2163 Fern Street
Eureka, CA 95503
USA
dalton.michael@sbcglobal.net

Geoff Pound
c/o HCT
PO Box 4114
FUJAIRAH,
United Arab Emirates
geoffpound@yahoo.com.au